Making a Good
MARRIAGE
Even Better

OTHER BOOKS BY DICK PURNELL

A 31-DAY EXPERIMENT

Making a Good
MARRIAGE
Even Better

DICK PURNELL

THOMAS NELSON PUBLISHERS

Nashville

Published in Nashville, Tennessee, by Thomas Nelson, Inc., Publishers, and distributed in Canada by Word Communications, Ltd., Richmond, British Columbia, and in the United Kingdom by Word (UK), Ltd., Milton Keynes, England.

Scripture quotations are taken from the HOLY BIBLE, NEW INTERNATIONAL VERSION ®. Copyright © 1973, 1978, 1984 by International Bible Society. Used by permission of Zondervan Bible Publishing House. All rights reserved.

The "NIV" and "New International Version" trademarks are registered in the United States Patent and Trademark Office by International Bible Society. Use of either trademark requires the permission of International Bible Society.

Library of Congress Cataloging-in-Publication Data

Purnell, Dick.
　　Making a good marriage even better / Dick Purnell.
　　　　p.　cm. — (A 31-day experiment)
　　ISBN 0-8407-4346-7
　　1. Married people-Prayer-books and devotions—English. 2. Devotional exercises. 3. Marriage—Religious aspects—Christianity. I. Title. II. Series: Purnell, Dick. 31-day experiment.
BV4596.M3P87 1994
248.8'44—dc20
　　　　　　　　　　　　　　　　　　　　　　　　93–37599
　　　　　　　　　　　　　　　　　　　　　　　　CIP

Printed in the United States of America
1 2 3 4 5 6 7 - 98 97 96 95 94

CONTENTS

TO MOM AND DAD

*For 42 years you worked at
building a strong marriage.
Thanks for the example you gave
to my wife Paula and me.*

FOUNDATION FOR A HAPPY HOME

Have you ever wondered how God plans for us, as imperfect human beings, to develop a satisfying and successful marriage?

The statistics on divorce, as well as on those who stay married but feel alienated from their spouses, show that many couples are having difficulties making it work. What's our problem? We have gotten off the foundation that the Creator of marriage has established for a happy home.

God has much to say on this subject in His Word. In fact, one of the most frequently repeated verses in the entire Bible is, "A man will leave his father and mother and be united to his wife, and they will become one flesh" (Genesis 2:24; see Matthew 19:5; 1 Corinthians 6:16; Ephesians 5:31).

God wants to emphasize something extremely important to His children. He created the institution of marriage so that a man and woman can experience intimate oneness with each other. But it must be done His way.

We face many challenges in today's culture that can tear the bonds of marriage and weaken the relationship between a husband and a wife. God's design for a happy home is often lost in the confusing pressures of daily life and the failures of marriages around us.

Since marriage was the Lord's idea in the first place, He has very significant instructions about how to make it work. The Bible says, "The fear of the LORD is the beginning of wisdom, and knowledge of the Holy One is understanding" (Proverbs 9:10).

A friend of mine is a partner in an international company. He is friendly and likes to help people. Recently he related to me that an employee of his talked with him about her marital troubles. She has been married for eighteen months, but is seeking a divorce. He told me that during their conversation about her marital troubles, she said several times, "All I want to be is happy."

People cannot make themselves happy by trying to orchestrate their lives to meet their own desires. Marital happiness is based upon understanding God's principles of marriage and applying them in the power of the Holy Spirit.

By wisdom a house is built, and through understanding it is established; through knowledge its rooms are filled with rare and beautiful treasures. (Proverbs 24:3-4)

It would be wonderful to have the kind of home where your relationship with your spouse is an intimate oneness which fills every aspect of your lives with rare and beautiful treasures. That kind of marital harmony is not only possible, but it is what God wants for you. Christ commanded, "So they are no longer two, but one. Therefore what God has joined together, let man not separate" (Matthew 19:6).

The only glue that can keep a husband and wife together and happy is our heavenly Father. His power is available to energize people to live the way He has instructed.

Unless the LORD builds the house, its builders labor in vain. (Psalm 127:1)

Do you want your marriage to be filled with the principles of God and energized by the Holy Spirit? Is it your desire to improve and strengthen your relationship with your mate?

This Experiment in *Making a Good Marriage Even Better* is designed to get you into God's Word and to get God's Word into you. As you try this Experiment, you will spend at least 30 minutes each day reading the passage for that day and applying its teaching to your life and marriage. From the very first day you will begin to learn how to build your home upon the eternal truths of God's Word.

The passages you will study are divided into two sections. The first is **Understanding God's Blueprint for Marriage.** There are many books written on marriage with a variety of suggestions and advice given by the authors. Some are good and some are not. But what about God's suggestions and advice? I have not included my ideas. You will study the Lord's statements and develop your own conclusions. There is no greater authority on marriage than God Himself!

The second section is **Strengthening the Ties That Bind.** In your marriage you will face many joys and sorrows as you encounter challenging circumstances. What are the instructions that God gives to handle life's situations? You will study 15 insightful passages that will give you guidance to develop a godly marriage through the ups and downs of daily living.

It is my hope that in one month you will cultivate a deeper relationship with your mate and with God, who made both of you for each other. The Bible says, "Taste and see that the LORD is good; blessed is the man who takes refuge in him" (Psalm 34:8). That is a magnificent invitation and challenge to experience all that God has in store for you.

Ask your mate to do the Experiment along with you. It would be an exciting 31 days of strengthening your relationship and enhancing your commitment to the Lord. Each day read the passage separately and write down your thoughts. The project at the end of each session gives exciting ideas to understand each other better. Put the lessons you have learned into practice using the simple guidelines given in the section entitled "Process for Developing Marital Oneness."

Before you go to bed at night, discuss with your mate the things you are learning and endeavoring to put into practice in your relationship. Pray with each other and for each other. End the day in thanksgiving to the Lord for all He is doing to bring you closer together.

May the heavenly Father unlock the mysteries of marriage for you. I pray that you and your mate will increasingly enjoy your relationship—not just for 31 days, but for the rest of your lives.

In His joy,

Dick

BIBLICAL PICTURE OF A MARRIAGE

To give you the wonderful picture of building a marriage as expressed in the Bible, here are 31 topics you will study for the next month.

Section 1: Understanding God's Blueprint for Marriage

1. The Main Ingredients in a Happy Marriage

2. Receiving Your Mate as God's Gift

3. Spiritual Oneness

4. Radical Transformation

5. Source of Power for a Strong Marriage

6. God's Plan for Marriage

7. Qualities of a Godly Husband

8. Decisive Leadership

9. A Woman of Excellence

MY PRAYER

Dear Heavenly Father,

Since You designed marriage, You know how to help me develop an exciting oneness with my mate, and to make it last a lifetime. Thank You for bringing us together.

My deepest desire is for our marriage to be the most fulfilling and exciting one that it can possibly be. Only You have the plan and power to make it work.

I place my marriage in Your hands. We are facing challenges and pressures that tend to pull us apart.

I need You. We need You. Give us Your wisdom and strength to develop our marriage on Your Word and to be filled with Your love.

Help me to know You more intimately and guide my mate and me to fulfill all Your desires for us as individuals and as a couple.

Build our marriage into all You want it to be. I am looking forward to the next month with great expectation and hope.

Signed _____

MY COVENANT
WITH GOD

    I commit myself before God to do this Experiment in Making a Good Marriage Even Better for the next 31 days. I make a covenant with the heavenly Father to:

1. Spend up to 30 minutes each day in Bible study, prayer, and writing out my thoughts and plans.

2. Encourage my mate to pray daily for me. (He/she may want to do the Experiment with you.)

3. Attend a church each week where the Word of God is taught.

Signed _____

Date   _____

PROCESS FOR DEVELOPING MARITAL ONENESS

A. **PREPARATION FOR EACH DAY**
   1. *Equipment:* Obtain a Bible to study and a pen to record your thoughts and plans in this book.
   2. *Time:* Choose a specific half-hour each day to spend with the Lord. Pick the time of day that is best for you—when your heart is most responsive to meeting with God.
   3. *Place:* Find a particular spot where you can clear your mind of distractions and focus your full attention on God's Word. Suggestions: bedroom, office, library, living room, lounge, outdoors.

B. **READ—20 Minutes**
   1. Pray earnestly before you begin. Ask the Lord to teach you what He wants you to learn.
   2. Read the entire passage.

3. Read it again, looking for important ideas.
4. Make written notes on the following:
   a. Questions A and B—Study the passage thoroughly to answer the questions. Observe what God says about Himself and how you can live a dynamic, godly life. As you discover more of His truth, your understanding of God's purposes for you and your marriage will increase.
   b. Section C—Decide how you will apply the teachings in the passage to your life.
5. Choose a verse from the passage you have read that is especially meaningful to you. Copy it onto a card and read it several times during the day. Think about its meaning and impact on your life. Memorize it when you have free mental time, for example, while you are getting ready in the morning, standing in line, taking a coffee break, walking somewhere, or relaxing in the evening.

C. NEED—5 Minutes
1. Choose what is the most pressing marital need you have as a couple. What will bring greater harmony and oneness in your relationship with your mate? Examples:
   a. spending more of your time together

     b. handling financial hardship

     c. resolving conflict with your spouse

     d. having patience with each other

     e. making an important decision

     f. calming your fears about something

     g. conquering recurring temptation

     h. accomplishing something

2. Write down your request. The more specific you are, the more specific the answer will be.

3. Earnestly pray each day for God's provision.

4. When the Lord meets your need, record the date and how He did it. Periodically review God's wonderful provisions, and thank Him often for His faithfulness. This will greatly increase your faith.

5. At the end of the month, review all the answers to your prayers. Rejoice in God's goodness to you. Keep praying for the requests that still need answers.

D. DEED—5 Minutes

1. Pray for God's guidance on how you can help your mate during that day. Try to apply the particular passage you have just studied.

2. Take the initiative to express God's wonderful love to your mate. Be a servant. Someone has

said, "Behind every face there is a drama going on." Tap into his or her drama.

3. As you work on strengthening your marriage, determine to grow in your relationship with Christ. Developing a strong faith in the Lord is the greatest goal in life.

4. Later, record the details of how the Holy Spirit used you this day. This will increase your confidence to trust God to develop other areas of your marriage. Thank the Lord Jesus for expressing His love and compassion through you.

E. PROJECTS

1. The key to enhancing your marriage is applying God's Word. Integrate what you learn from the passage you studied into your daily life. It will take hard work, but your marriage will grow stronger as you and your mate put God's truth into practice.

2. Make a commitment to do the projects. Schedule a time during the day to work on them, and trust the Lord for the wisdom to make His truths a vital part of your marriage.

3. Start a **Marriage-Builder Notebook**. Each day enter the projects you are working on. Add ideas and questions you come up with. Do additional

study in areas that are the most interesting and helpful for you.

F. **LAST THING IN THE EVENING**
    1. **READ** the passage again, looking for additional facts about God and about His ideas for strengthening your marriage.
    2. Pray again for your **NEED**. Thank the Lord that He will answer in His way and in His time.
    3. Record the **DEED** God guided you to accomplish.
    4. Review the **PROJECT** you and your mate have worked on during the day. Finish anything left to be done before you go to sleep.

G. **PARTNERS**
    Ask your mate to do the Experiment with you. Pray frequently for each other that you will learn more about the Lord and how to develop a marriage built on His Word. Encourage one another to be disciplined and faithful in completing the Experiment. Set aside time each day to share what you are learning and pray together for God's power to unite your lives together in His love. Help each other to apply what you are learning.

THE EXPERIMENT

31 Days

of

Making a Good Marriage Even Better

Section 1
Understanding God's
Blueprint for Marriage
Days 1-16

THE MAIN INGREDIENTS IN A HAPPY MARRIAGE

Psalm 128:1–6

KEY VERSES:
Blessed are all who fear the LORD, who walk in his ways.
You will eat the fruit of your labor; blessings and prosperity will be yours (Psalm 128:1–2).

TODAY'S FOCUS:
To fear the Lord means a person "stands in awe" of Him and honors Him. When a person has an intimate relationship with God, it produces wonderful results in his/her marriage through the joys and sorrows of life.

READ:
Pray to walk in God's ways.

A. When a person fears the Lord, what will He do for that individual?

B. How will walking in God's ways affect your marriage?

C. My heart attitude toward the Lord is:

NEED:
Pray to walk in His ways.

Our greatest need today is:

God answered my prayers today _____ (date) in this way:

DEED:
Thank the Lord for His blessings on your marriage.

Lord, work in my family by:

▲

PROJECT:
How would it change your life if you trusted God more deeply and consistently? How would it change your relationship with your spouse?

RECEIVING YOUR MATE AS GOD'S GIFT

Genesis 2:15–25

KEY VERSE:

For this reason a man will leave his father and mother and be united to his wife, and they will become one flesh (Genesis 2:24).

TODAY'S FOCUS:

It is wonderful that God created man and woman to be suited for each other. He established your marriage and gave you your mate—specially designed for you.

READ:

Pray for a receptive attitude.

A. God made Adam and Eve to be suitable for each other. What was Adam's response when God brought Eve into his life?

B. What were they to do as a couple? (Also look at Genesis 1:26–31.)

C. God gave me my spouse. My response is:

NEED:

Pray for oneness with your mate.

    Our greatest need today is:

    God answered my prayers today _____ (date) in this way:

DEED:

Thank God you are one flesh with your mate.

    Dear Lord, I want to show my love and appreciation to my spouse by:

▲

PROJECT:

Review your wedding vows. Write down all the ways your spouse has completed you. Express appreciation by sharing those things with her/him.

SPIRITUAL ONENESS

Psalm 95:1–7

▼

KEY VERSES:
Come, let us bow down in worship, let us kneel before the LORD our Maker; for he is our God and we are the people of his pasture, the flock under his care (Psalm 95:6–7).

TODAY'S FOCUS:
In a marriage, spiritual oneness bonds the two of you together. Your commitment to God will enhance your commitment to each other.

READ:
Pray for mutual commitment to God.

A. Invite your mate to worship the Lord with you. What are some ways you can praise Him together?

B. In Psalm 34:1–3 how can you individually and as a couple worship God?

C. I thank God for:

NEED:

Thank God that He cares for you both.

Our greatest need today is:

God answered my prayers today _____ (date) in this way:

DEED:

Praise the Lord together for His greatness.

Dear God, teach me and my mate to:

▲

PROJECT:

Plan a worship time with just your mate. Write down everything you are thankful to God for. Sing songs that express your feelings about the Lord. Thank Him that your marriage is under His care.

RADICAL TRANSFORMATION

Ephesians 2:1–10

KEY VERSES:

But because of his great love for us, God, who is rich in mercy, made us alive with Christ even when we were dead in transgressions—it is by grace you have been saved (Ephesians 2:4–5).

TODAY'S FOCUS:

If you have put your faith in Christ, you are a different person. The new you can bring positive changes to your marriage relationship.

READ:

Pray that God will change you.

A. When an individual is self-reliant and without a personal relationship with God, he/she has the following characteristics:

B. Faith in Christ results in changes. What are they?

C. I know God has made me alive with Christ because:

NEED:

Thank the Lord for His grace.

Our greatest need today is:

God answered my prayers today _____ (date) in this way:

DEED:

Thank God for His great love for you and your mate.

Dear Lord, give me the power to do good works toward my mate. Guide me to:

▲

PROJECT:

Make a list of the specific changes God has brought in your life since you gave your life to Christ. How have these changes affected your relationship with your spouse?

SOURCE OF POWER FOR A STRONG MARRIAGE

Ephesians 5:15–20

KEY VERSES:
Therefore do not be foolish, but understand what the Lord's will is. Do not get drunk on wine, which leads to debauchery. Instead, be filled with the Spirit (Ephesians 5:17–18).

TODAY'S FOCUS:
To be filled with the Holy Spirit means to trust Him to empower you to live as God wants you to live. He is the source of power for your marriage.

READ:
Pray for wisdom.

A. In this passage, what are some characteristics of a Spirit-filled life?

B. What else will the Holy Spirit do for believers? (Read John 16:5–15.)

C. I trust the Holy Spirit to empower me to:

NEED:

Pray for the Spirit to guide you.

Our greatest need today is:

God answered my prayers today _____ (date) in this way:

DEED:

Thank God that the Holy Spirit lives in you.

Dear Father, give me the opportunity to:

▲

PROJECT:

The Holy Spirit lives inside each believer (Romans 8:9–17). But does He fill (control) your life? If not, confess your sins to God and ask Him by faith to control and empower you. Ask Him to bring your spouse to the same commitment.

GOD'S PLAN FOR MARRIAGE

Ephesians 5:21–33

▼

KEY VERSE:
Submit to one another out of reverence for Christ (Ephesians 5:21).

TODAY'S FOCUS:
The foundation of a good marriage is for both husband and wife to be filled with the Spirit and submit to each other. That's God's plan—and it works!

READ:
Pray for greater commitment to God's plan.

A. What are the responsibilities of a husband toward his wife?

B. What are the responsibilities of a wife toward her husband?

C. My response to this passage is:

NEED:

Pray for your mate to do what God commands.

Our greatest need today is:

God answered my prayers today _____ (date) in this way:

DEED:

Thank God for your mate.

Today, I want to do something special for my spouse. This is what I will do:

▲

PROJECT:

Discuss these issues with your spouse:

1. What does it mean for the husband to be head of his wife and to love her as Christ loved the church?
2. What does it mean for the wife to submit to her husband and to respect him? (Read 1 Corinthians 11:3.)
3. How can you apply these principles to one current decision you are facing in your marriage?

QUALITIES OF A GODLY HUSBAND

1 Timothy 3:1–13

KEY VERSE:
He must manage his own family well (1 Timothy 3:4).

TODAY'S FOCUS:
The qualities of a Christian leader (overseer and deacon) also apply to a Christian husband—the leader of his family. A godly marriage requires action from both husband and wife.

READ:
Pray for insight.

A. To be a Christian leader, what qualities does God want a man to possess?

B. How would having these qualities affect your marriage?

C. Husband: I want to develop the following qualities:

Wife: Because I desire to be a "woman worthy of respect," I will:

NEED:

Pray for a good reputation with outsiders.

    Our greatest need today is:

    God answered my prayers today _____ (date) in this way:

DEED:

Pray to manage your marriage well.

    Husband: This is what I will do for my wife today:

    Wife: I want to encourage my husband by:

▲

PROJECT:

Husband: Ask a trusted friend to evaluate your life in reference to the qualities discussed in this passage. In which areas are you doing well? Where do you need to grow? Pray often and work hard to improve.

Wife: Encourage your husband in one specific, special way today. Do it in love and with humility and sensitivity to his feelings.

DECISIVE LEADERSHIP

Joshua 23:14–24:15

▼

KEY VERSE:

But if serving the LORD seems undesirable to you, then choose for yourselves this day whom you will serve, whether the gods your forefathers served beyond the River, or the gods of the Amorites, in whose land you are living. But as for me and my household, we will serve the LORD (Joshua 24:15).

TODAY'S FOCUS:

God is faithful. The man who leads his marriage by faithfully serving the Lord will see the fulfillment of what God has promised.

READ:

Pray for courage.

A. Joshua had led Israel into the Promised Land. At the end of his life, he reminded his people of God's faithfulness. Why did he do that?

B. How did he demonstrate decisive leadership?

C. Husband: I will lead my wife by:

Wife: I will follow my husband's leadership by:

NEED:

Choose to serve the Lord regardless of what others do.

    Our greatest need today is:

    God answered my prayers today _____ (date) in this way:

DEED:

Thank God for His faithfulness.

    Lord, help me to be strong and decisive in order to:

▲

PROJECT:

Start a Book of Memories together. Write down specific things God has done in your lives before you were married and afterward. How does He want you to live in the future?

A WOMAN OF EXCELLENCE

Proverbs 31:10–31

KEY VERSE:
Charm is deceptive, and beauty is fleeting; but a woman who fears the LORD is to be praised (Proverbs 31:30).

TODAY'S FOCUS:
Forget the world's definition of what it means to be a wife. In God's eyes, the praiseworthy wife is a godly wife. She is a woman of noble character with rare and magnificent qualities.

READ:
Pray for discernment.

A. What are some character qualities that this woman displayed?

B. What effect does she have on her husband?

C. My response to this passage is:

NEED:

Pray to bring honor to your mate.

Our greatest need today is:

God answered my prayers today _____ (date) in this way:

DEED:

Pray for strength to do what God wants you to do.

Wife: This is what I will do today for my husband:

Husband: This is how I will communicate appreciation to my wife for her qualities:

▲

PROJECT:

What are the underlying character qualities that this woman's activities reveal? Choose one or two of these qualities to work on in the next month to improve your life. Remember the greatest of all is to fear the Lord (v. 30). Trust Him for the wisdom and power to become what He wants you to be.

GIVING A BLESSING

1 Peter 3:1–12

▼

KEY VERSES:

Wives, in the same way be submissive to your husbands.
. . . Husbands, in the same way be considerate as you live
with your wives (1 Peter 3:1, 7).

TODAY'S FOCUS:

Being kind toward your mate is God's design for the
relationship between husband and wife. This will result
in your receiving a blessing—individually and as a couple.

READ:

Pray for harmony with your spouse.

A.   How can a wife be a blessing to her husband?

B.   How can a husband be a blessing to his wife?

C.   I want my marriage to be characterized by:

NEED:

Pray to love life and see good days.

Our greatest need today is:

God answered my prayers today _____ (date) in this way:

DEED:

Pray for compassion and humility toward your mate.

I want to be a blessing to my spouse by:

▲

PROJECT:

Discuss together the meanings of the following and how to apply them to your marriage:

1. Gentle and quiet spirit.
2. Submission to your husband.
3. Treat your wife with respect.
4. Don't repay insult with insult.
5. Inherit a blessing.
6. Seek peace and pursue it.

LOVE THAT DEEPLY SATISFIES

1 Corinthians 13:1–13

KEY VERSE:
And now these three remain: faith, hope and love. But the greatest of these is love (1 Corinthians 13:13).

TODAY'S FOCUS:
Regardless of your success in life, God wants you to emphasize loving your mate in His way. This kind of love is the love that deeply satisfies.

READ:
Pray to be filled with God's love.

A. Explain God's definition of *love*.

B. How does this passage help enhance your love for your spouse?

C. I want my love to be characterized by:

NEED:

Pray for God's power to love.

Our greatest need today is:

God answered my prayers today _____ (date) in this way:

DEED:

Pray to be patient, kind, and humble.

Dear Father, fill me with Your kind of love so that:

▲

PROJECT:

Evaluate yourself by inserting your name into each description of love in this passage. For example: "(Your name) is patient," "(Your name) is kind," and so on. Devise a plan to improve in at least one area that fails to measure up to the love described in this passage.

*Date*_____

LEARNING TO LOVE LIKE GOD

1 John 4:7–21

▼

KEY VERSES:
Dear friends, since God so loved us, we also ought to love one another. No one has ever seen God; but if we love one another, God lives in us and his love is made complete in us (1 John 4:11–12).

TODAY'S FOCUS:
True love comes from God! Understanding how He loves will help you love your mate unconditionally, sacrificially, and wholeheartedly.

READ:
Pray for God's love to characterize your life.

A. What are the ingredients of love? How can you love your mate?

B. How does God demonstrate that He loves you and your mate?

C. I want my love for my mate to be characterized by:

NEED:
Ask God to remove any fear you may have of loving your mate.

Our greatest need today is:

God answered my prayers today _____ (date) in this way:

DEED:
Pray for unselfishness.

Lord, because You live in me, I ask You to:

▲

PROJECT:
One way God demonstrates His love is by always taking the initiative toward us. Think of one or two ways you can take the initiative to show love toward your mate. Do something special—write a love poem, compose a romantic song, praise him/her, give something unique.

UNDERSTANDING SEXUAL INTIMACY

1 Corinthians 7:1–7

▼

KEY VERSES:

The husband should fulfill his marital duty to his wife, and likewise the wife to her husband. The wife's body does not belong to her alone but also to her husband. In the same way, the husband's body does not belong to him alone but also to his wife (1 Corinthians 7:3–4).

TODAY'S FOCUS:

Sexual intimacy within marriage is a joyful privilege given by God. A marital relationship on this level is to be desired, respected, and protected.

READ:

Pray for sensitivity.

A. Sexual intimacy within marriage is a joyful privilege given by God. How does the Lord want a married couple to relate sexually to each other?

B. What does the Bible mean when it states: "Marriage should be honored by all, and the marriage bed kept pure" (Hebrews 13:4)?

C. My response to this passage is:

NEED:
Pray that you will fulfill your mate's sexual needs.

Our greatest need today is:

God answered my prayers today _____ (date) in this way:

DEED:
Thank God for the sexual intimacy you share with your mate.

Lord, lead me to show my mate:

▲

PROJECT:
Discuss with your mate how you "own" each other's body. Ask what her or his sexual needs are and how you can fulfill them.

ENJOYING SEXUAL INTIMACY

Song of Songs 7:1–9

▼

KEY VERSE:
How beautiful you are and how pleasing, O love, with your delights! (Song of Songs 7:6).

TODAY'S FOCUS:
One of the pleasures of being married is enjoying each other romantically. Physical attraction and fulfillment between spouses is God-designed!

READ:
Pray for romantic pleasure with your mate.

A. The writer enjoys his lover. What attracted him to her?

B. The beloved woman wrote romantic thoughts about him in the Song of Songs 5:10–16. How did she describe her feelings about him?

C. This is what attracts me to my mate:

NEED:

Pray for deeper love.

Our greatest need today is:

God answered my prayers today _____ (date) in this way:

DEED:

Thank God for your mate.

I will show my mate how much I love her/him in this way:

▲

PROJECT:

How would you describe your romantic feelings toward your mate? Write a love letter to your mate expressing your attraction to her/him. Either mail it or give it at a romantic time.

INGREDIENTS OF MARITAL HARMONY

Philippians 2:1–11

▼

KEY VERSES:

Do nothing out of selfish ambition or vain conceit, but in humility consider others better than yourselves. Each of you should look not only to your own interests, but also to the interests of others (Philippians 2:3–4).

TODAY'S FOCUS:

Geniune humility produces a sincere concern for others and their needs. Giving your spouse's needs priority develops marital harmony.

READ:

Pray for mutual commitment to harmony.

A. What are the factors in developing oneness between a husband and wife?

B. Why is Christ's example of humility so important for marital harmony?

C. Because I want to build unity with my mate, I will:

NEED:
Pray for humility.
   Our greatest need today is:

   God answered my prayers today _____ (date) in this
   way:

DEED:
Pray to become interested in your mate's interests.

▲

PROJECT:
Review these ingredients of harmony. What are the greatest hindrances to oneness with your mate? How can you overcome them?
   Write yourself a letter about these issues. Reread it in a week or two to see how you are doing in improving your relationship.

THE SPIRIT-BUILT MARRIAGE

Galatians 5:13–26

KEY VERSES:
The fruit of the Spirit is love, joy, peace, patience, kindness, goodness, faithfulness, gentleness and self-control. Against such things there is no law (Galatians 5:22–23).

TODAY'S FOCUS:
A marriage under the influence of the Holy Spirit can't help but produce the fruit of the Spirit. And who would not want those qualities in a relationship?

READ:
Pray to serve each other in love.

A. Compare the results of self-centeredness and Spirit-centeredness.

Acts of the sinful nature	Fruit of the Spirit

B. How do these attitudes and actions affect my marriage?

C. I want my marriage to be filled with the fruit of the Spirit because:

NEED:

Pray to produce the fruit of the Spirit in your life and marriage.

Our greatest need today is:

God answered my prayers today _____ (date) in this way:

DEED:

Pray to be led by the Spirit each day.

One fruit of the Spirit I want to emphasize is:

▲

PROJECT:

Discuss with your mate the fruit of the Spirit. How can these qualities be improved within your marriage? Encourage each other to live by the Spirit and daily keep in step with Him.

THE EXPERIMENT

31 Days

of

Making a
Good Marriage
Even Better

Section 2
Strengthening the
Ties That Bind
Days 17 - 31

A DYSFUNCTIONAL MARRIAGE

Genesis 27:1–46

KEY VERSE:
[Rebekah] said to him, "My son, let the curse fall on me. Just do what I say" (Genesis 27:13).

TODAY'S FOCUS:
Deceit and lies have no place in a marriage. They will only lead to disharmony and ultimately destruction.

READ:
Pray for sensitivity to the Lord.

A. It was the custom in Isaac's day to give the eldest son a blessing, something like an inheritance near the end of a father's life. How did Rebekah, Isaac's wife, feel about her son Esau receiving the blessing? What did she do about it?

B. How did her attitude and actions affect her family?

C. Because I want my marriage to reflect a different perspective, I will:

NEED:
Pray for victory over destructive attitudes and actions.
   Our greatest need today is:

   God answered my prayers today _____ (date) in this way:

DEED:
Pray to remove any falsehood from your marriage.
   Lord, help me to encourage my spouse by:

▲

PROJECT:
Do you like Isaac and Rebekah's marriage? Why? How can you prevent similar attitudes and actions from destroying your marriage?

THE NEW YOU

Colossians 3:1–11

▼

KEY VERSES:

Since, then, you have been raised with Christ, set your hearts on things above, where Christ is seated at the right hand of God. Set your minds on things above, not on earthly things (Colossians 3:1–2).

TODAY'S FOCUS:

When Christ changes you, He changes your marriage. Happy is the couple whose hearts and minds are set on God-given priorities.

READ:

Thank God for your new life in Christ.

A. God has given commands so that your marriage relationship will be the most rewarding.

Avoid these things:	Do these things:

B. Why should you focus on the "things above"?

C. Because I have been raised with Christ, I will:

NEED:
Pray to set your heart on things above.
   Our greatest need today is:

   God answered my prayers today _____ (date) in this
   way:

DEED:
Pray to set your heart on things above.
   In my marriage, I need to:

▲

PROJECT:
Ask your spouse how you both can work on eliminating
the negative aspects in your marriage. Change the negative things that are sin in God's eyes. Ask God for His
strength to become what He wants you to be.

BECOMING ONE WITH YOUR MATE

Colossians 3:12–21

▼

KEY VERSE:

And whatever you do, whether in word or deed, do it all in the name of the Lord Jesus, giving thanks to God the Father through him (Colossians 3:17).

TODAY'S FOCUS:

Because you are one of God's chosen people, He has given you guidelines for your marriage. Becoming one with your mate takes hard work, but it is worth the effort.

READ:

Pray for understanding.

A. What attitudes and actions will bring you closer to your spouse?

B. What should a husband do? What should a wife do?

C. With God's guidance in mind, I will:

NEED:

Pray to forgive your mate as the Lord forgave you.

Our greatest need today is:

God answered my prayers today _____ (date) in this way:

DEED:

Thank God the Father for all He has done for you.

Because I want to clothe myself with compassion, kindness, humility, gentleness, and patience toward my mate, I will:

▲

PROJECT:

Compare your marriage with the guidelines given in this passage. Choose the top two areas to focus on today. Work at them with all your heart, giving thanks to the Lord.

UNDERSTANDING YOUR MATE'S DIFFERENCES

Romans 12:1–8

KEY VERSES:

Just as each of us has one body with many members, and these members do not all have the same function, so in Christ we who are many form one body, and each member belongs to all the others (Romans 12:4–5).

TODAY'S FOCUS:

Learn to appreciate the differences in each other. Each of you has been given unique talents, abilities, and gifts—all to be used to God's glory.

READ:

Pray for a renewed mind.

A. A successful marriage is built on both the husband and the wife being transformed. Why is this true?

B. List the different gifts given in the passage. What should a person do with his/her gifts?

C. I offer myself as a living sacrifice to God because:

NEED:

Pray for God's will in your life and marriage.

Our greatest need today is:

God answered my prayers today _____ (date) in this way:

DEED:

Pray to understand your mate's gifts.

Dear Lord, help me to encourage my spouse to:

▲

PROJECT:

Study the different spiritual gifts in these passages: Romans 12:3–8; 1 Corinthians 12:1–11; Ephesians 4:11–13. Which gifts do you and your spouse have? How could they be used for God's glory? Determine to encourage each other to develop and refine those gifts.

BEING DEVOTED TO ONE ANOTHER

Romans 12:9–21

KEY VERSE:

Be devoted to one another in brotherly love. Honor one another above yourselves (Romans 12:10).

TODAY'S FOCUS:

Love is more than an emotion. It involves being devoted to each other. The qualities of true loving devotion cover a wide range of life's circumstances.

READ:

Pray to cling to what is good.

A. Write out three of these commands that you feel need the most attention in your marriage. If you both applied them, how would your relationship be improved?

B. What are some ways to deal with difficult circumstances?

C. When I want to honor my mate, I will:

NEED:
Pray to live at peace with each other.
Our greatest need today is:

God answered my prayers today _____ (date) in this
way:

DEED:
Pray to fervently serve the Lord together.
Lord, give me the strength and wisdom to:

▲

PROJECT:
Put the commands in this passage onto a chart with four
sections entitled: **Relating to 1. God; 2. Yourself; 3. Your
Mate; 4. Others.** How would you develop each of these
areas? What other biblical comments would you include?

GROWING THROUGH TOUGH TIMES

James 1:1–18

▼

KEY VERSES:

Consider it pure joy, my brothers, whenever you face trials of many kinds, because you know that the testing of your faith develops perseverance (James 1:2–3).

TODAY'S FOCUS:

Every marriage will encounter pressures, trials, temptations, and problems. It's important to the health of your relationship to learn to handle the tough times God's way.

READ:

Pray for wisdom in handling trials and temptations.

A. When tough times come, what does God encourage you to do?

B. When you handle these trials in God's way, what happens in your life?

C. When I encounter trials and temptations, I will:

NEED:

Pray for unwavering faith.

Our greatest need today is:

God answered my prayers today _____ (date) in this way:

DEED:

Thank God that He gives you wisdom.

Lord, today I trust You to:

▲

PROJECT:

God has given us wonderful promises to help us grow through tough times. Study them with your mate so you can apply them to your circumstances. Some promises are found in 2 Corinthians 1:3–7; 4:7–18; 12:9–10; 1 Peter 1:3–9; 4:12–19. Claim one verse together, memorize it, and use it as an encouragement tool when you face the next trial.

CONFIDENCE IN CONQUERING HARDSHIPS

Romans 8:26–39

▼

KEY VERSE:
And we know that in all things God works for the good of those who love him, who have been called according to his purpose (Romans 8:28).

TODAY'S FOCUS:
You can be confident that even during the hardships you experience as a couple, God is still in control. He's still at work, and He wants to help you through.

READ:
Pray for God's purposes to be completed in your marriage.

A. When you encounter hardships as a couple, what has
   God promised you?

B. How do you know that the Lord will never stop
   loving you?

C. I thank God for:

NEED:

Thank God you are more than a conqueror because of Christ's love for you.

Our greatest need today is:

God answered my prayers today _____ (date) in this way:

DEED:

Thank the Lord for the Holy Spirit's intercession.

Dear God, fill me with Your strength so that:

▲

PROJECT:

What are some hardships you have faced as a couple? Write down the lessons the Lord has taught you through them. How can you trust Him in current challenges? Discuss today possible solutions and pray about them together.

TOGETHERNESS IN HANDLING DIFFICULTIES

1 Samuel 1:1–28

▼

KEY VERSE:
But to Hannah he gave a double portion because he loved her, and the LORD had closed her womb (1 Samuel 1:5).

TODAY'S FOCUS:
Difficulties are to be faced *together*. Tender actions and kind words during the tough times will draw you closer to each other and to the Lord.

READ:
Pray for confidence when facing problems.

A. Even though the social custom of his time was to have more than one wife, Elkanah had a strong relationship with Hannah. How did they show their love for each other?

B. How did their faith in God pull them through a very difficult situation?

C. I will look to God in difficult times by:

NEED:

Worship the Lord regardless of your circumstances.

Our greatest need today is:

God answered my prayers today _____ (date) in this way:

DEED:

Pray for greater trust in God.

Lord Almighty, help me to encourage my mate to grow in his or her faith in You by:

▲

PROJECT:

What is the most difficult situation you are facing? Together study Joshua 1:1–9 about God's faithfulness and strength to help you overcome that difficulty. Meditate on the Lord's promises that encourage you to trust Him for solutions. Agree on one step you can take today to help each other.

GOD'S INTERVENTION

1 Samuel 2:1–11

KEY VERSE:
My heart rejoices in the LORD; in the LORD my horn is lifted high (1 Samuel 2:1).

TODAY'S FOCUS:
God answers prayer! He is alive and active in your life, in your marriage, and in the tough times.

READ:
Praise God for who He is.

A. Hannah was grateful for God's wonderful provision. She praised the Lord for His actions toward her and other needy people. How does He help them?

B. How else did God provide for Elkanah and Hannah (1 Samuel 2:18–21)?

C. My heart rejoices in the Lord also, because:

NEED:
Trust God for what He will do.

Our greatest need today is:

God answered my prayers today _____ (date) in this way:

DEED:
Praise God for what He has done for you and your mate.

Lord, there is no one like You. Give us strength to:

▲

PROJECT:
With your mate, look back on all the answers to prayers you have received so far while doing this Experiment. Praise God for each of those answers and pray for the needs yet to be fulfilled.

OVERCOMING SEXUAL TEMPTATION

1 Corinthians 6:9–20

▼

KEY VERSES:

Do you not know that your body is a temple of the Holy Spirit, who is in you, whom you have received from God? You are not your own; you were bought at a price. Therefore honor God with your body (1 Corinthians 6:19–20).

TODAY'S FOCUS:

Because He loves us, God has set boundaries on our behavior. God clearly prohibits sexual immorality. We can overcome sexual temptations through God's power.

READ:

Pray for understanding.

A. Sexual immorality is having intimate sexual contact with someone who is not your marriage partner. Why is it wrong in God's eyes?

B. How can you overcome temptation to do something immoral?

C. I am committed to God's perspective on sexual immorality because:

NEED:
Pray for His power.
Our greatest need today is:

God answered my prayers today _____ (date) in this way:

DEED:
Thank God that the Holy Spirit is in you.
Lord, help me to:

▲

PROJECT:
Write down the main ideas you find in the following passages about this topic: Proverbs 7:1–27; 9:13–18; Romans 13:13–14; Galatians 5:16–21; Ephesians 4:17–24; Colossians 3:5–10; 1 Thessalonians 4:1–8.

If you have problems in this area, confess your sin to the Lord, trust Him for the power to change, and refuse to give in to temptation in the future.

HANDLING CONFLICT

Ephesians 4:17–32

▼

KEY VERSES:
Get rid of all bitterness, rage and anger, brawling and slander, along with every form of malice. Be kind and compassionate to one another, forgiving each other, just as in Christ God forgave you (Ephesians 4:31–32).

TODAY'S FOCUS:
Every couple will face disagreements and friction. How you deal with them will either draw you together or tear you apart.

READ:
Pray for new attitudes.

A. What are some positive things you can do to handle conflict?

B. What are some negative things you can stop doing?

C. This is what I will do when I have a conflict with my mate:

NEED:

Pray to be kind and compassionate.

Our greatest need today is:

God answered my prayers today _____ (date) in this way:

DEED:

Pray to forgive as God has forgiven you.

Because I don't want to grieve the Holy Spirit, I will:

▲

PROJECT:

Discuss with your mate your top three areas of conflict. What can you do to resolve the problems? Choose at least one step you can take to solve the strife.

FORGIVENESS

Matthew 18:21–35

▼

KEY VERSES:

Then Peter came to Jesus and asked, "Lord, how many times shall I forgive my brother when he sins against me? Up to seven times?" Jesus answered, "I tell you, not seven times, but seventy-seven times" (Matthew 18:21–22).

TODAY'S FOCUS:

Hurt and misunderstandings are inevitable in a marital relationship. To maintain harmony and deepen intimacy, forgiveness is essential.

READ:

Pray for a forgiving attitude.

A. Instead of holding grudges, sulking with anger, or seeking revenge, forgive your mate. Why does Christ want you to do this?

B. Read Matthew 5:23–24 and Mark 11:25. Who needs forgiveness and who should take the initiative?

C. When I don't feel like forgiving my mate, I will:

NEED:
Pray for reconciliation.
 Our greatest need today is:

 God answered my prayers today _____ (date) in this
way:

DEED:
Thank God He has forgiven you.
 Heavenly Father, give me the strength to:

▲

PROJECT:
With your mate, study these additional passages about
forgiving each other: Matthew 6:12–15; Luke 15:11–32;
17:1–6; Ephesians 4:31–32; and Colossians 3:12–13. In
what areas do you need to forgive your mate? In what areas
do you need to be forgiven? Take the initiative to restore
your relationship to oneness.

HOW TO FIGHT WITH YOUR REAL ENEMY

Ephesians 6:10–20

▼

KEY VERSES:
Put on the full armor of God so that you can take your stand against the devil's schemes. For our struggle is not against flesh and blood, but against the rulers, against the authorities, against the powers of this dark world and against the spiritual forces of evil in the heavenly realms (Ephesians 6:11–12).

TODAY'S FOCUS:
Satan is opposed to your marriage. He will do his best to create conflict, chaos, and disunity in your relationship with your spouse. The devil, not your mate, is your real enemy.

READ:
Pray to be strong in the Lord.

A. From Ephesians 5:18 to 6:9 Paul wrote about family and business relationships. Now he urges us to put on the full armor of God. Describe each piece of the armor.

B. Since your mate is not your real enemy, how can you use the armor of God to stand together against the devil?

C. When battles with my mate arise, I will:

NEED:

Pray for God's mighty power.

Our greatest need today is:

God answered my prayers today _____ (date) in this way:

DEED:

Pray for all the saints (believers in Christ).

Lord, as my mate and I utilize the armor of God, we want You to:

▲

PROJECT:

Together with your mate, study more about each piece of God's armor. Suggest how you can use each one to strengthen your marriage and to fight together against the real enemy. Pray sitting knee to knee, holding hands and forming a circle of two, standing firm together in the power of God against the real enemy.

MAKING YOUR MARRIAGE COUNT FOR ETERNITY

Acts 18:1–4, 18–28

▼

KEY VERSE:
When Priscilla and Aquila heard him, they invited him to their home and explained to him the way of God more adequately (Acts 18:26).

TODAY'S FOCUS:
As a married couple, you can have a significant eternal impact on those around you. Together your influence for Christ will affect many other people.

READ:
Pray for kindness and hospitality.

A. Aquila and Priscilla had a profound impact on two men. Who were the men and how did they help them?

B. Look at Romans 16:3–5, 1 Corinthians 16:19, and 2 Timothy 4:19. What else did they do?

C. I want my mate and me to have an impact for Christ because:

NEED:

Pray for courage to witness.

Our greatest need today is:

God answered my prayers today _____ (date) in this way:

DEED:

Pray for opportunities to help others learn about Christ.

Lord, give us boldness and strength to:

▲

PROJECT:

Talk with your mate about getting involved in reaching people for Christ. Ask your pastor how you can help him spread the gospel. Seek opportunities to get involved in building others in the faith. Plan one time within the next month that you can host some people in your home. Show them love and hospitality. Share with them your faith in Christ.

THE SOURCE OF HAPPINESS

Psalm 145:1–21

▼

KEY VERSES:
Great is the LORD and most worthy of praise; his greatness no one can fathom. One generation will commend your works to another; they will tell of your mighty acts (Psalm 145:3–4).

TODAY'S FOCUS:
Happiness comes from a thankful attitude for all God's provisions, regardless of the circumstances you are facing. Be thankful for one of God's greatest gifts to you—your mate!

READ:
Praise God for His abundant goodness to you.

A. Now that you're at the end of this Experiment, it is important to focus again on the Lord and His greatness. What has God done in your life and marriage?

B. What would you like the next generation to know about the Lord?

C. I exalt my God the King for:

NEED:
Pray that God will fulfill your deepest desires.
Our greatest need today is:

God answered my prayers today _____ (date) in this
way:

DEED:
Thank God for His faithfulness to all His promises.
I want to show my gratefulness to God by:

▲

PROJECT:
With your mate, make a tape recording of the mighty acts
of God in your lives and relationship. Talk about how He
brought you together and what He has done to mold you
into one, especially during the days you have been doing
this Experiment. At the end of the tape, thank the Lord
for His goodness and faithfulness. Date the tape and
replay it together in six months for a special evening of
remembering God's provisions for you. If you have children, let them listen to it also.

CELEBRATION!

Congratulations! You did it. You have finished a whole month of working through the Word of God, studying the Lord's statements and instructions about building a strong marriage. During the process there were many challenges to grow personally and to develop a deeper oneness with your mate.

Don't stop now. Continue to work on applying the things you have learned. In the next section I have included **Resources for Your Marriage: Practical Advice from Proverbs** which lists wise advice from one of the wisest men who ever lived: Solomon. He was inspired by the Lord to write insights and instructions that will guide you to handle the challenges of living with another human being who is different from you.

Read a proverb a day and try to incorporate its teachings into your personal life, marriage, and occupation. Memorize the verses that are especially meaningful to you.

I've also included a section called **Additional 31-Day Experiments**, which describes other month-long Experiments you can try. Choose one that will meet your needs and help you develop your faith in Christ. Make a habit of spending at least 30 minutes each day studying God's Word, praying, and communicating with the heavenly Father.

Keep moving forward. Trust the Holy Spirit to reveal the truths God wants you to know and apply to your life and marriage. Wisdom comes from living out what God has put into your heart. Remember God's promise:

> By wisdom a house is built, and through understanding it is established; through knowledge its rooms are filled with rare and beautiful treasures. (Proverbs 24:3-4)

RESOURCES FOR YOUR MARRIAGE: PRACTICAL ADVICE FROM PROVERBS

Solomon asked God for wisdom to lead his country in the ways of the Lord. As a result, he was given great understanding into human nature and how best to live life. He wrote the book of Proverbs to give God's instructions about many things, including marriage.

Below are God's instructions for building yourself up as well as building a strong relationship with your mate. While Solomon was indeed wise, he did eventually stray from God's truths; beware of his example. His life and kingdom ended in shambles. Learn from his mistakes. Take these wise sayings and trust the Lord to give you the power to apply them to your life and marriage for as long as you live. If you do that, you will make a good marriage even better.

BUILDING MATERIALS FOR A MAXIMUM MARRIAGE

18:22   He who finds a wife finds what is good and receives favor from the LORD.

12:4   A wife of noble character is her husband's crown, but a disgraceful wife is like decay in his bones.

20:6   Many a man claims to have unfailing love, but a faithful man who can find?

31:10   A wife of noble character who can find? She is worth far more than rubies.

5:18–19   May your fountain be blessed, and may you rejoice in the wife of your youth. A loving doe, a graceful deer—may her breasts satisfy you always, may you ever be captivated by her love.

15:6   The house of the righteous contains great treasure, but the income of the wicked brings them trouble.

19:14   Houses and wealth are inherited from parents, but a prudent wife is from the LORD.

FACTORS IN A QUALITY RELATIONSHIP

24:3–4   By wisdom a house is built, and through understanding it is established; through knowledge its rooms are filled with rare and beautiful treasures.

3:33   The LORD's curse is on the house of the wicked, but he blesses the home of the righteous.

14:1   The wise woman builds her house, but with her own hands the foolish one tears hers down.

20:7   The righteous man leads a blameless life; blessed are his children after him.

15:17   Better a meal of vegetables where there is love than a fattened calf with hatred.

17:1   Better a dry crust with peace and quiet than a house full of feasting, with strife.

31:30   Charm is deceptive, and beauty is fleeting; but a woman who fears the LORD is to be praised.

21:21   He who pursues righteousness and love finds life, prosperity and honor.

| 3:3–4 | Let love and faithfulness never leave you; bind them around your neck, write them on the tablet of your heart. Then you will win favor and a good name in the sight of God and man. |

11:30   The fruit of the righteous is a tree of life, and he who wins souls is wise.

15:33   The fear of the LORD teaches a man wisdom, and humility comes before honor.

15:8   The LORD detests the sacrifice of the wicked, but the prayer of the upright pleases him.

THREATS TO A MARRIAGE

27:8   Like a bird that strays from its nest is a man who strays from his home.

27:15–16 A quarrelsome wife is like a constant dripping on a rainy day; restraining her is like restraining the wind or grasping oil with the hand.

17:13   If a man pays back evil for good, evil will never leave his house.

21:9   Better to live on a corner of the roof than share a house with a quarrelsome wife.

21:19   Better to live in a desert than with a quarrelsome and ill-tempered wife.

26:20–21   Without wood a fire goes out; without gossip a quarrel dies down. As charcoal to embers and as wood to fire, so is a quarrelsome man for kindling strife.

30:33   For as churning the milk produces butter, and as twisting the nose produces blood, so stirring up anger produces strife.

29:22   An angry man stirs up dissension, and a hot-tempered one commits many sins.

26:28   A lying tongue hates those it hurts, and a flattering mouth works ruin.

12:13   An evil man is trapped by his sinful talk, but a righteous man escapes trouble.

18:13   He who answers before listening—that is his folly and his shame.

16:18   Pride goes before destruction, a haughty spirit before a fall.

16:5   The LORD detests all the proud of heart. Be sure of this: They will not go unpunished.

14:30   A heart at peace gives life to the body, but envy rots the bones.

WISDOM TO BUILD A MARRIAGE ON

9:10   The fear of the LORD is the beginning of wisdom, and knowledge of the Holy One is understanding.

4:7   Wisdom is supreme; therefore get wisdom. Though it cost all you have, get understanding.

8:10–11   Choose my instruction instead of silver, knowledge rather than choice gold, for wisdom is more precious than rubies, and nothing you desire can compare with her.

23:23   Buy the truth and do not sell it; get wisdom, discipline and understanding.

11:2   When pride comes, then comes disgrace, but with humility comes wisdom.

19:8   He who gets wisdom loves his own soul; he who cherishes understanding prospers.

2:1–8   My son, if you accept my words and store up my commands within you, turning your ear to wisdom and applying your heart to understanding, and if you call out for insight and cry aloud for understanding, and if you look for it as for silver and search for it as for hidden treasure, then you will understand the fear of the LORD and find the knowledge of God. For the LORD gives wisdom, and from his mouth come knowledge and understanding. He holds victory in store for the upright, he is a shield to those whose walk is blameless, for he guards the course of the just and protects the way of his faithful ones.

24:14 Know also that wisdom is sweet to your soul; if you find it, there is a future hope for you, and your hope will not be cut off.

16:16 How much better to get wisdom than gold, to choose understanding rather than silver!

RESOLVING CONFLICTS

15:1 A gentle answer turns away wrath, but a harsh word stirs up anger.

17:9 He who covers over an offense promotes love, but whoever repeats the matter separates close friends.

15:18 A hot-tempered man stirs up dissension, but a patient man calms a quarrel.

20:3 It is to a man's honor to avoid strife, but every fool is quick to quarrel.

20:22	Do not say, "I'll pay you back for this wrong!" Wait for the LORD, and he will deliver you.
19:11	A man's wisdom gives him patience; it is to his glory to overlook an offense.
12:18	Reckless words pierce like a sword, but the tongue of the wise brings healing.
16:6	Through love and faithfulness sin is atoned for; through the fear of the LORD a man avoids evil.
28:13	He who conceals his sins does not prosper, but whoever confesses and renounces them finds mercy.
17:27	A man of knowledge uses words with restraint, and a man of understanding is even-tempered.
10:19	When words are many, sin is not absent, but he who holds his tongue is wise.
13:3	He who guards his lips guards his life, but he who speaks rashly will come to ruin.
17:14	Starting a quarrel is like breaching a dam; so drop the matter before a dispute breaks out.

29:11   A fool gives full vent to his anger, but a wise man keeps himself under control.

ENCOURAGING YOUR MATE

25:11   A word aptly spoken is like apples of gold in settings of silver.

16:21-24   The wise in heart are called discerning, and pleasant words promote instruction. Understanding is a fountain of life to those who have it, but folly brings punishment to fools. A wise man's heart guides his mouth, and his lips promote instruction. Pleasant words are a honeycomb, sweet to the soul and healing to the bones.

15:30   A cheerful look brings joy to the heart, and good news gives health to the bones.

20:15   Gold there is, and rubies in abundance, but lips that speak knowledge are a rare jewel.

15:23   A man finds joy in giving an apt reply—and how good is a timely word!

12:25   An anxious heart weighs a man down, but a kind word cheers him up.

12:14   From the fruit of his lips a man is filled with good things.

| 10:11 | The mouth of the righteous is a fountain of life, but violence overwhelms the mouth of the wicked. |

THE ART OF GOOD COMMUNICATION

| 24:26 | An honest answer is like a kiss on the lips. |

| 18:21 | The tongue has the power of life and death, and those who love it will eat its fruit. |

| 12:22 | The LORD detests lying lips, but he delights in men who are truthful. |

| 14:29 | A patient man has great understanding, but a quick-tempered man displays folly. |

| 10:31 | The mouth of the righteous brings forth wisdom, but a perverse tongue will be cut out. |

| 15:2 | The tongue of the wise commends knowledge, but the mouth of the fool gushes folly. |

| 15:4 | The tongue that brings healing is a tree of life, but a deceitful tongue crushes the spirit. |

| 16:13 | Kings take pleasure in honest lips; they value a man who speaks the truth. |

HOW TO MAKE RIGHT DECISIONS

3:5–6   Trust in the LORD with all your heart and lean not on your own understanding; in all your ways acknowledge him, and he will make your paths straight.

16:9   In his heart a man plans his course, but the LORD determines his steps.

19:21   Many are the plans in a man's heart, but it is the LORD's purpose that prevails.

16:3   Commit to the LORD whatever you do, and your plans will succeed.

21:30   There is no wisdom, no insight, no plan that can succeed against the LORD.

20:18   Make plans by seeking advice; if you wage war, obtain guidance.

14:22   Do not those who plot evil go astray? But those who plan what is good find love and faithfulness.

21:3   To do what is right and just is more acceptable to the LORD than sacrifice.

12:2   A good man obtains favor from the LORD, but the LORD condemns a crafty man.

15:9	The LORD detests the way of the wicked but he loves those who pursue righteousness.
10:27	The fear of the LORD adds length to life, but the years of the wicked are cut short.
12:28	In the way of righteousness there is life; along that path is immortality.
3:7	Do not be wise in your own eyes; fear the LORD and shun evil.

SECURITY IN TOUGH TIMES

18:10	The name of the LORD is a strong tower; the righteous run to it and are safe.
14:26–27	He who fears the LORD has a secure fortress, and for his children it will be a refuge. The fear of the LORD is a fountain of life, turning a man from the snares of death.
19:23	The fear of the LORD leads to life: Then one rests content, untouched by trouble.
12:7	Wicked men are overthrown and are no more, but the house of the righteous stands firm.
30:5	Every word of God is flawless; he is a shield to those who take refuge in him.

16:7	When a man's ways are pleasing to the LORD, he makes even his enemies live at peace with him.
23:17–18	Do not let your heart envy sinners, but always be zealous for the fear of the LORD. There is surely a future hope for you, and your hope will not be cut off.
29:25	Fear of man will prove to be a snare, but whoever trusts in the LORD is kept safe.
2:6–8	For the LORD gives wisdom, and from his mouth come knowledge and understanding. He holds victory in store for the upright, he is a shield to those whose walk is blameless, for he guards the course of the just and protects the way of his faithful ones.
28:26	He who trusts in himself is a fool, but he who walks in wisdom is kept safe.

HOW TO GET AND GIVE WISE ADVICE

16:20	Whoever gives heed to instruction prospers, and blessed is he who trusts in the LORD.
19:20	Listen to advice and accept instruction, and in the end you will be wise.

9:9   Instruct a wise man and he will be wiser still; teach a righteous man and he will add to his learning.

13:14   The teaching of the wise is a fountain of life, turning a man from the snares of death.

15:31   He who listens to a life-giving rebuke will be at home among the wise.

12:15   The way of a fool seems right to him, but a wise man listens to advice.

25:12   Like an earring of gold or an ornament of fine gold is a wise man's rebuke to a listening ear.

BENEFITS OF GOOD FRIENDSHIPS

27:17   As iron sharpens iron, so one man sharpens another.

18:24   A man of many companions may come to ruin, but there is a friend who sticks closer than a brother.

17:17   A friend loves at all times, and a brother is born for adversity.

13:20   He who walks with the wise grows wise, but a companion of fools suffers harm.

27:5–6   Better is open rebuke than hidden love.
          Wounds from a friend can be trusted, but an
          enemy multiplies kisses.

27:9   Perfume and incense bring joy to the heart,
          and the pleasantness of one's friend springs
          from his earnest counsel.

HANDLING SEXUAL TEMPTATION

2:16–19   (Wisdom) will save you also from the adul-
          teress, from the wayward wife with her se-
          ductive words, who has left the partner of her
          youth and ignored the covenant she made
          before God. For her house leads down to
          death and her paths to the spirits of the dead.
          None who go to her return or attain the
          paths of life.

5:3–6   For the lips of an adulteress drip honey, and
          her speech is smoother than oil; but in the
          end she is bitter as gall, sharp as a double-
          edged sword. Her feet go down to death; her
          steps lead straight to the grave. She gives no
          thought to the way of life; her paths are
          crooked, but she knows it not.

6:23–29   For these commands are a lamp, this teach-
          ing is a light, and the corrections of discipline

are the way to life, keeping you from the immoral woman, from the smooth tongue of the wayward wife. Do not lust in your heart after her beauty or let her captivate you with her eyes, for the prostitute reduces you to a loaf of bread, and the adulteress preys upon your very life. Can a man scoop fire into his lap without his clothes being burned? Can a man walk on hot coals without his feet being scorched? So is he who sleeps with another man's wife; no one who touches her will go unpunished.

ADDITIONAL
31-DAY
EXPERIMENTS

GROWING CLOSER TO GOD

Do you want to develop a deeper oneness with the Lord? This book is designed to cultivate your relationship with God by looking at passages that will help you discover truths that are foundational to knowing the Lord intimately. You'll learn about His purpose and plan for you and about how to be transformed from the inside out.

A PERSONAL EXPERIMENT IN
FAITH-BUILDING

Begin to see your confidence in God develop into a more consistent trust. Your faith will grow as you learn to apply God's Word to your life and expect Christ to accomplish great things through you. You will never be the same as you discover how Christ built the faith of His disciples.

STANDING STRONG IN A GODLESS CULTURE

Try this Experiment and find out what it takes to walk powerfully with God and hold onto biblical values regardless of society's pressures. It will help you develop strength for your personal needs, wisdom to make tough choices, and courage to face complex problems.

KNOWING GOD'S HEART, SHARING HIS JOY

Find your special place in God's heart and eternal plan. Gain a clearer insight into God's life-changing message for all people. As a result, you will learn to become a more effective witness for Christ. By understanding God's heart, you'll be freed to share the plan of salvation with others—naturally and easily.

BUILDING A POSITIVE SELF-IMAGE

Would you like to improve your self-image? You can become all that God wants you to be. This book will help you develop a biblical self-image as you look into God's Word and see your worth in His eyes. You will discover new harmony, purpose, and direction for your life.

KNOWING GOD BY HIS NAMES

Spend 31 days discovering how God has revealed Himself through His names. Each name gives you significant insight into His character and how He meets your needs. Learn how the Heavenly Father provides for you, the Prince of Peace calms your anxiety, the Shepherd guides you, and many other ways God relates to you through His names.

BUILDING A STRONG FAMILY

Who has the best advice for raising children? God does! You will study the biblical passages that reveal God's commands and advice for developing your children in a way that pleases Him—and will please you, too. As you put into practice God's principles on parenting, your family will notice the difference.

ABOUT THE
AUTHOR

Dick Purnell is the founder and director of **Single Life Resources**, a ministry of Campus Crusade for Christ. In addition, he is an internationally known speaker and author.

A graduate of Wheaton College, Dick holds a Master of Divinity degree from Trinity Evangelical Divinity School and a master's degree in education (specializing in counseling) from Indiana University.

Dick is the author of *Becoming a Friend and Lover, Free to Love Again: Coming to Terms with Sexual Regret,* and *Building a Relationship That Lasts.* He has also written eight books in the *31-Day Experiment* series.

Dick and Paula have two daughters, Rachel and Ashley. They love living in North Carolina.